The Fiverr Seller's Handbook

EASY STEPS TO MAKE MONEY ONLINE

BUDDLEWRITER

Learn The Secrets To Becoming A Top Fiverr Seller And Earning Consistent Income Each Month!

KAREN BLAIR

THE FIVERR SELLER'S HANDBOOK: EASY STEPS TO MAKE MONEY ONLINE
Learn The Secrets To Becoming A Top Fiverr Seller And Earning Consistent Income Each Month!

For permission, special orders, corporate sales, etc., please contact the author at kaywillwrite@gmail.com or the publisher at info@buddlewriter.com.

ISBN: 978-1-932448-34-4 (paperback). Also Available in eBook

Published by BuddleWriter
Kingston, Jamaica.
www.buddlewriter.com

BUDDLEWRITER

Preface

Hey,

Making money online has never been easier or more exciting! The Fiverr Seller's Handbook: Easy Steps To Make More Money Online is a step-by-step guide to unlocking the world of Fiverr and achieving real financial freedom.

In the pages ahead, I'll take you through **a step-by-step journey to making money on Fiverr**. I'll provide tips and tricks that the top Fiverr Sellers use to get consistent orders and earn consistent income every month. Plus, I'll share with you some of my best-kept secrets for achieving success on Fiverr - things that even many experienced sellers don't know about!

This guide is designed to make working on Fiverr fun, exciting, and, most importantly, easy. To start making money online today, all you need is guidance and an action plan. I'm here to provide both for you. With this book, you'll have everything at your fingertips to become a successful Fiverr Seller.

Stop worrying about how to pay for the things you love. Unlock your true potential and start saying **YES** to more of life's opportunities. This book is your opportunity to do just that. **With this guide, making money on Fiverr will be easy, fun, and lucrative! Get started now and reap the rewards soon - financial freedom awaits.**

Happy selling, Let's get started!

Your Fiverr Coach,

Karen

Table of Contents

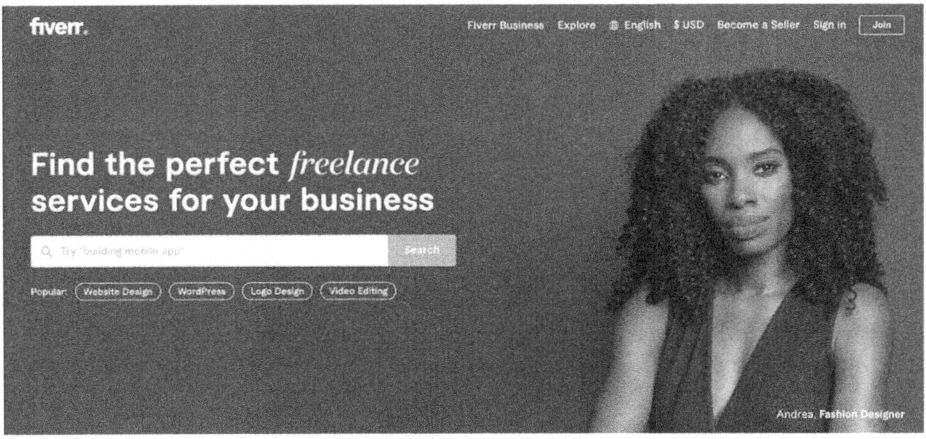

CHAPTER 1

What is Fiverr?

FIVERR IS A GLOBAL ONLINE MARKETPLACE offering tasks and services, referred to as 'gigs,' for as little as $5. Jobs offered on the site include writing, translation, graphic design, video editing, and programming.

Fiverr is one of the most popular sites for people looking to outsource work online and has been growing steadily since it was founded in 2010. Headquartered in Tel Aviv, Israel, Fiverr has become a go-to site for small businesses and entrepreneurs looking to get quality work done quickly and affordably. It's also become a popular platform for freelancers to find work and build their portfolios.

Can I Join Fiverr Free?

Yes, you can join Fiverr for free as a Buyer or a Seller. As a Seller, you can sign up and create your gigs for free. Once your gigs are live, you can start receiving orders from buyers.

As a Buyer, you can browse through the available gigs and purchase the ones you need. You will only be charged for the gig once you are satisfied with the work delivered by the Seller.

Is Fiverr Safe For Freelancers, and Can I Trust it to Get Paid?

Yes, Fiverr is a safe platform for freelancers to find work and get paid. All payments on Fiverr are processed through PayPal or direct bank transfer, so you can be sure your money is secure.

In addition, Fiverr offers a buyer protection program that covers orders against non-delivery or if the work delivered does not match the gig description.

- ★ The platform is easy to use and has a user-friendly interface.
- ★ Fiverr offers great payment protection for freelancers, so you can be sure you'll get paid for your work.
- ★ Fiverr is a great way to build your portfolio and get exposure to a large audience of potential clients.
- ★ The site attracts high-quality buyers who are willing to pay for quality work.
- ★ Fiverr is a great way to supplement your income as a freelancer.

CHAPTER 2

How Does Fiverr Work?

B**EFORE WE GET INTO THE PLATFORM'S PROCESSES**, let's simplify some terms you'll need to know.

Gigs: Fiverr services are called *"gigs."* They are what you offer to your buyers on Fiverr.

Buyers: People who come to Fiverr to buy gigs are called *"buyers."* They browse through the gig catalog, and purchase gigs that they feel will help them with their project.

Sellers: You, the person offering the gigs on Fiverr, are referred to as a *"seller."*

Orders: When a buyer purchases one of your gigs, it is referred to as an *"order."*

Custom offer: If you and a buyer negotiate a price for a gig that is different from the one listed on Fiverr, it is referred to as a *"custom offer."*

Warnings: Fiverr may issue you a warning if they feel you are violating their terms of service. If you receive three warnings, your account will be suspended.

Extras: Extras are additional services you can offer buyers for an additional fee. They are a great way to upsell your services and make more money on Fiverr.

Now that we have those out of the way, let's get into how Fiverr works.

The Buyer's Journey

When buyers come to Fiverr, they have a problem they need to solve. It is your job, as a seller, to offer them a gig that will solve their problem.

The buyer will browse through the available gigs and purchase the one they feel will best help them with their project. Once the gig is purchased, the buyer and seller will communicate through the Fiverr platform to discuss the project details.

The buyer will then provide you with all the necessary information and files to complete the gig. Once you have everything, you will start working on the project.

Once you have completed the project, you will upload it to the Fiverr platform for the buyer to review. If the buyer is happy with the work, they will approve it and leave you a positive review.

If the buyer is unhappy with the work, they may request revisions or cancel the order. It is essential to try to satisfy the buyer's needs so that you can avoid cancellations and negative reviews.

The Seller's Journey

Now that we have covered the buyer's journey, let's look at the seller's journey on Fiverr.

As a seller, you will need to create gigs offering services you are qualified to provide. When creating your gigs, it is important to be clear and concise in your gig descriptions.

You should also include high-quality images and videos in your gig to help it stand out from the competition. Once you have created your gigs, it is time to start marketing them to buyers.

There are several ways that you can market your gigs on Fiverr. You can share them on social media, post them in relevant forums, or even run ads.

The more buyers see your gigs, the more likely you are to make sales. Once you start receiving orders, it is important to deliver quality work and communicate well with your buyers.

If you do a good job, you will receive positive reviews and repeat buyers. If you deliver quality work and provide great customer service, you will be successful on Fiverr.

Fiverr Revenue Model

Fiverr has a very straightforward revenue model. For every gig you sell and complete, your account is credited with revenue equal to 80% of the purchase amount. So, if you sell a gig for $5, you will earn $4 in revenue.

This system is designed to incentivize both buyers and sellers to create high-quality gigs that deliver value. By ensuring that both parties are satisfied with the transaction, Fiverr can create a sustainable marketplace that everyone can benefit from.

Of course, this revenue model also benefits Fiverr itself. By taking a 20% cut of every transaction, Fiverr can generate a healthy amount of revenue while still providing its users with an excellent platform to buy and sell services.

With this business model, Fiverr has quickly become one of the most popular online marketplaces, showing no signs of slowing down.

Fiverr Seller Levels

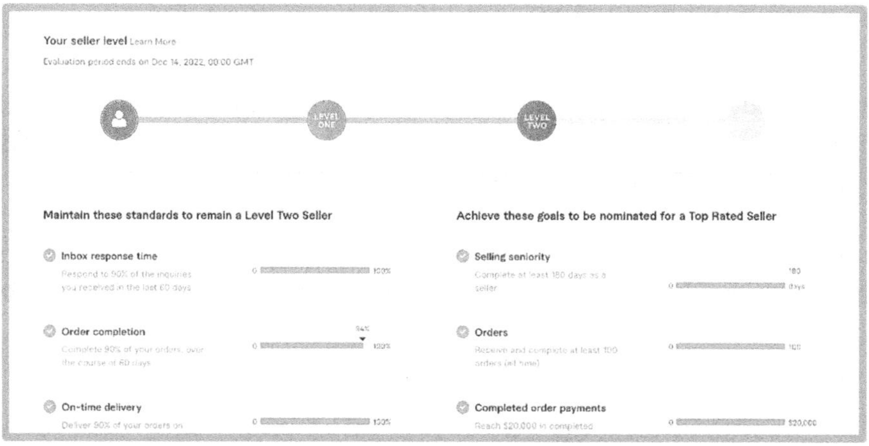

Your success level on Fiverr each month will determine your Seller level. By providing great customer service, maintaining high buyer satisfaction, and timely delivery, you can reach the top-level status on Fiverr, which gets you more orders and traffic.

As you complete more and more orders on Fiverr, you'll start to move up through the Seller levels. There are four Seller levels on Fiverr, and each level comes with its own set of benefits that can help you succeed on the platform.

The four Seller levels are:

New Seller

As a beginner, you are automatically labeled a New Seller. Sellers in this category can:

- Create up to 7 active Gigs (services)
- Add 2 extra services per Gig
- Create custom offers up to $20,000 each
- Withdraw earnings after 14 days

Level 1

To get to this level, new Sellers must meet the following requirements:

- Be an active Seller for at least 60 days
- Completed at least 10 orders
- Earned a minimum of $400
- Maintained at least a 4.7-star rating
- Have a response time of at least 90% (this has to do with how long you take to respond to clients)
- Delivered work on-time at least 90% of the time over the 60 days
- Received no warnings over 30 days regarding violation of the Terms of Service (TOS).

As a Level 1 Seller, you can:

- Create up to 10 Gigs
- Add up to 4 Gig extras per Gig
- Create custom offers up to $20,000 each
- Withdraw your earnings after 14 days

Level 2

To get to this level, Level 1 Sellers must:

- Be an active seller for at least 120 days
- Have completed at least 50 orders
- Have earned at least $2000
- Be maintaining at least a 4.7-star rating
- Have a response rate of at least 90%
- Have an Order completion score of 90% and above
- Have received no TOS warnings

Moving from Level 1 to Level 2 is an automatic process. As a Level 2 Seller, you can:

- Create up to 20 active Gigs
- Add up to 5 Gig Extras per Gig
- Create custom offers up to $20,000 each
- Enjoy priority Customer Support
- Withdraw your earnings after 14 days

Top-Rated Seller

Top-Rated Sellers are the best of the best. This select group has distinguished themselves from their peers through exceptional performance on Fiverr and maintains a perfect score rating (meaning 0% negative reviews). This rating, however, is not automatic. Fiverr's editorial team manually reviews your performance for the previous 60 days and awards you this level when you meet the following requirements:

- Be an active seller for at least 180 days
- Have completed 100 orders or more
- Have earned more than $20,000
- Be maintaining at least a 4.7-star rating
- Have a response rate of at least 90%
- Have an Order completion score of 90% and above
- Have received no TOS warnings

As a Top-Rated Seller, you enjoy:

- up to 30 active Gigs
- up to 6 Gig extras per Gig
- Custom orders up to $20,000 each
- Priority Customer Service Support
- Withdrawing your earnings after 7 days

To maintain your status as a Top-Rated Seller, you must keep up your performance levels and meet the abovementioned requirements. If you fall below the standards, you will be moved back to Level 2 Seller.

CHAPTER 3

Deciding What To Sell On Fiverr

ONE OF THE MOST COMMON QUESTIONS I GET ASKED IS, *"what should I sell on Fiverr?"*

Figuring out what services you can offer that people are actually willing to pay for can be a challenge, especially if you're just starting out.

In this chapter, I'm going to share with you **5 simple ways** that you can use to figure out what to sell on Fiverr, as well as some popular services that people are already selling successfully.

1. **Look at what other people are selling:**

One of the easiest ways to figure out what services you can offer on Fiverr is to look at what other people are already selling and see if there's anything you can do that's similar.

To do this, go to www.fiverr.com and use the search bar to find services related to what you're interested in selling. For example, if you want to sell social media services, you can search for terms like *"social media marketing,"* *"Twitter marketing,"* or *"Instagram marketing."*

Once you've found a service, you could offer, look at the gig description and see what the person is offering. This will give you a good idea of what people are willing to pay for and help you come up with your own ideas for services that you can offer.

2. **Look at your existing skills and experience:**

Another great way to come up with ideas for services you can offer on Fiverr is to look at your existing skills and experience.

Think about the things you're good at and the kind of work you enjoy doing. Are there any skills or experience that you have that other people might be willing to pay for?

For example, if you're good at organizing or making phone calls and have a lot of experience doing it, you could offer your services as a virtual assistant or project manager. Or, if you're good at writing, you could offer your services as a copywriter or ghostwriter.

3. **Ask people what they need help with:**

Another great way to come up with ideas for services you can offer on Fiverr is to simply ask people what they need help with.

You can do this by talking to your friends, family, and co-workers or by joining relevant online communities and forums (such as **Reddit**) and asking people what kind of services they would be interested in.

4. Check out job boards:

Job boards can be a great source of inspiration for figuring out what to sell on Fiverr.

Go to www.freelancer.com or www.upwork.com and search for terms related to your skills and experience. For example, if you're good at writing, you could search for terms like *"freelance writer," "content writer," "blog writer,"* or *"copywriter."*

This will give you a good idea of the kind of services people are looking for and help you come up with your own ideas for services that you can offer.

5. Learn a skill on Skillshare:

If you're struggling to come up with ideas for services you can offer on Fiverr, another great option is learning a new skill on Skillshare.

Skillshare is an online learning platform that offers thousands of courses on various topics. And, best of all, many of the courses are free!

So, if you need help with ideas for services that you can offer on Fiverr, why not look at Skillshare and see if there's anything you can learn that could help you out?

Fiverr offers over 200 categories of services that you can offer, so finding something to sell isn't hard.

Some popular services that people are selling on Fiverr by category:

Writing & Translation:

- Articles
- Blog posts
- Stories
- Songs or Poems
- CV's
- Press releases
- Legal documents
- Essays
- Descriptions
- Reviews
- Proofreading & Editing
- Social media captions
- Speeches
- Taglines or Slogans
- Transcription
- Scripts
- Adverts
- Emails

Design:

- Logo
- Graphic design
- Video editing and animation
- Book cover design
- 3D modeling and rendering
- Social media posts
- Illustrations
- Infographics
- Photo editing (background removal)
- Game design
- Slideshows
- Newsletters
- Business cards

Digital Marketing:

- Search engine optimization (SEO)
- Social media marketing
- Web Analytics
- Content creation and curation
- Email campaigns
- Paid advertising and promotion

Business

- Consulting services
- Virtual Assistance
- Phone calls
- Data entry
- Research and surveys
-
- Customer service
- Recruiting
- Bookkeeping
- Market analysis

Music & Audio:

- Voiceovers
- Music lessons
- Audio editing and mixing
- Songwriting
- Sound effects creation
- Record voicemails

Lifestyle:

- Life coach
- Nutrition advice
- Fitness trainer
- Yoga and meditation
- Relationship advice

Programming & Tech:

- Web page editing
- Website development
- Build and customize WordPress themes
- Remove errors
- Install WordPress
- Website SEO
- Database development
- Web hosting
- User testing
- E-commerce
- Convert Files

So, there you have it – **five (5) tips to help you come up with great ideas for services you can offer on Fiverr!**

With the right combination of skills and experience and a bit of creativity, you can create a successful Fiverr business that will help you to make money online.

CHAPTER 4

How To Withdraw Payment From Fiverr

FIVERR OFFERS 3 PAYMENTS OPTIONS:

1. PayPal
2. Bank Transfer
3. Fiverr Revenue Card

Bank Transfer and Fiverr Revenue Card are linked to Payoneer. Payoneer is a secure online payment processor allowing users to make payments to other members or receive funds securely.

Before you can withdraw any funds from Fiverr, you must create and link either your Payoneer or PayPal account to your Fiverr account.

PayPal is not available in many countries, so if PayPal is not supported in your country, then you must use Bank Transfer or Fiverr Revenue Card (Payoneer).

How To Create A Payoneer Account

You will need the following to sign up:

- A bank account and your branch code.
- A National ID, Driver's License, or Passport.
- Email, Phone Number, and current Mailing Address.

Step 1: Go to Payoneer.com to create an account.

Step 2: Click on the Sign-Up and Earn $25.

Step 3: Select 'Freelancer or SMB' then 'Get paid by international clients or freelance marketplaces'

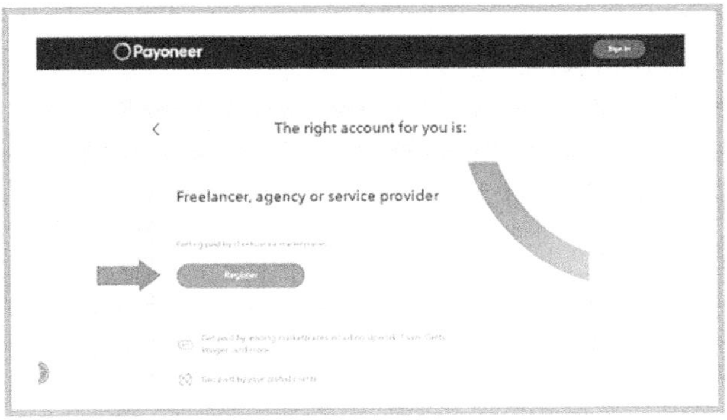

Step 4: Next, click Register

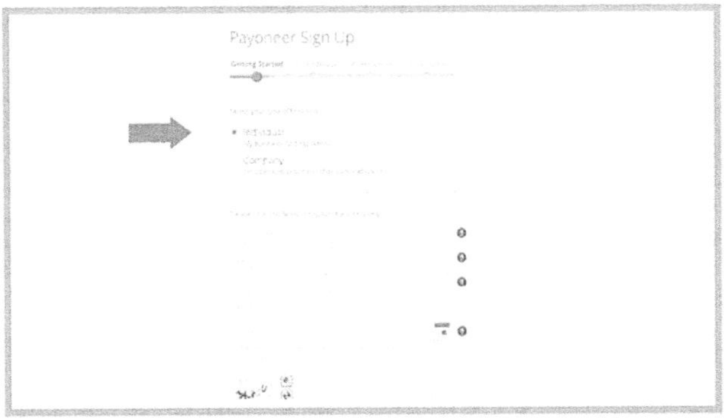

Step 5: Select the Individual option. Fill in the required details. Click Next.

Step 6: On the next screen, continue entering your details, including your phone number

- Note that this number can be used later to retrieve a forgotten password or update details.
- You'll receive a verification code on that mobile phone number.
- Simply enter the verification code with a 30 seconds time limit. Then click Next.

Step 7: Complete typing your details and ID requirements

Step 8: Enter your banking details

Step 9: Agree to the terms and click *'Submit'*

And that's it! Your application is submitted and now in review.

After 3 business days, you'll receive a confirmation of the review.

How To Link Your Payoneer Account to Fiverr

- From your Withdrawals page on Fiverr, choose either Bank transfer or Fiverr Revenue Card (this is only if you have a Payoneer Mastercard).
- You'll receive an email that directs you to Payoneer.
- Open the email and follow the links to enter your Payoneer username and password.
- You'll get a confirmation email letting you know that your accounts are linked.

You can now withdraw funds directly from your Fiverr balance page to your Payoneer Mastercard, which serves as your Fiverr Revenue card. Alternatively, you can transfer the funds through Payoneer directly to your bank account.

How To Create A PayPal Account:

1. Go to www.paypal.com and click Sign Up.
2. Select Sign Up for a Personal Account.
3. Enter your country, email address, and password.
4. Enter your other personal details.
5. Link your credit card to PayPal (optional).
6. Link your bank account to PayPal (optional).

7. Verify your email address with PayPal.

How To Link Your PayPal Account To Fiverr:

1. Go to your Fiverr dashboard. Click *My Business > Earnings*.

2. In the *WITHDRAW* area, click *PayPal Account.*

3. A notification will appear—indicating the withdrawal process has started, and you will receive an email.

4. Please note: Once you receive the email, you will need to define a PayPal account.

5. To continue with the process of setting up your PayPal account, click the link in the email. You will be redirected to Fiverr.

6. From the Configure Your PayPal Account page, in the PAYPAL ID (EMAIL ADDRESS) field, enter the email address associated with your PayPal account. Then, re-enter the address in the next field.

7. Select the *I UNDERSTAND AND AGREE* checkbox.

8. Click *CONNECT TO PAYPAL.*

9. A verification email is sent to the PayPal email you added for withdrawals. Please check your email and follow the instructions.

CHAPTER 5

How Do I Create A Fiverr Account?

NOW THAT YOU KNOW WHAT FIVERR IS AND HOW IT WORKS, you might be wondering how you can get started selling your services on the platform. In this chapter, I'll walk you through creating a Fiverr account step-by-step.

Getting started as a freelancer on Fiverr is FREE! By default, all accounts created on Fiverr are Buyer accounts. Therefore, you would create your Buyer account and then activate your Seller account.

Note!

- Activating your seller account is only available through your desktop.
- Creating your Gig is only available through your desktop.

To Create Your Fiverr Account:

1. Go to www.fiverr.com and click ***Join***.

Source: Fiverr.com

2. Next, enter your email address and click ***Continue***. You can choose to join with Facebook, Google Connect, or Apple Connect, but I strongly suggest using your email address.

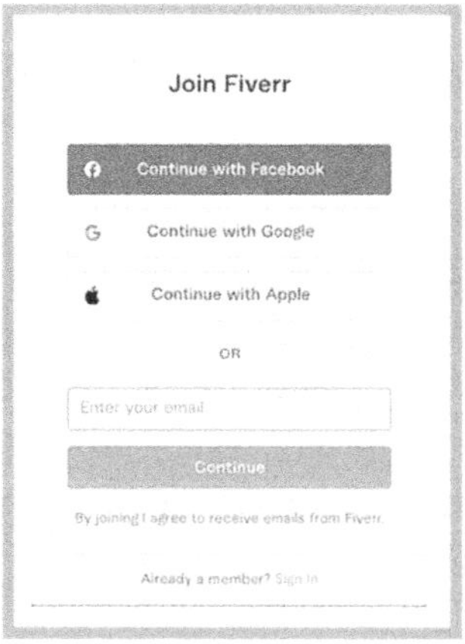

Source: Fiverr.com

3. Choose your username. Once you create your username, you **<u>CANNOT</u>** change it. This will be your display name and will be shown in your Fiverr URL. Therefore, think carefully about the name you use. Aim to be professional and include a word that describes the main service you want to be known for on Fiverr.

   For example, if you're a designer and most of your Gigs will focus on design, your username could be DesignGee. Your Fiverr URL would then become: www.fiverr.com/designgee

4. Decide on your password and then click ***Join***.

5. You are now a registered Fiverr user! Fiverr will send you an email to activate your account. Activate your account as quickly as possible, as the link in the email is only valid for 30 days after registration.

6. Within the activation email you receive from Fiverr, click ***Activate Your Account.***

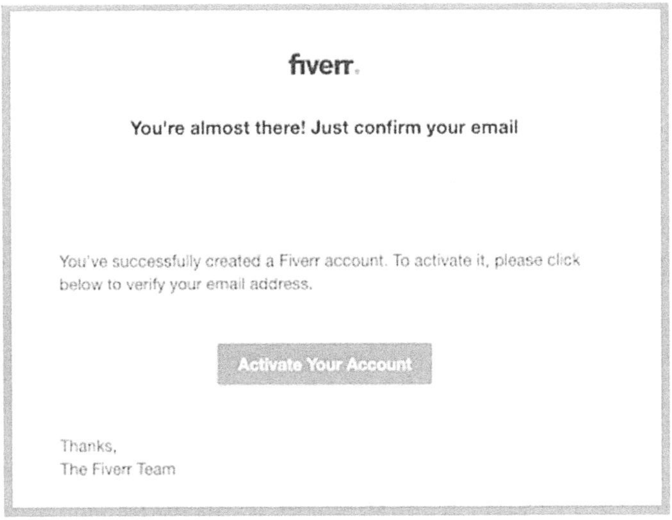

Source: Fiverr.com

Now that you have successfully created your account, it's time to activate your Seller's account to start offering services and earning money.

Activate Your Seller's Account

1. Click on your profile picture and select Become a Seller from the dropdown menu.

Source: Fiverr.com

2. You will be redirected to a homepage. From here, click on Become a Seller again to start the process. Three videos on How to use Fiverr as a seller will appear. Your screen should look like this:

   When you're through watching the videos, click Continue. You will be directed to tips on What makes a successful Fiverr profile and what to avoid as a seller. Click Continue.

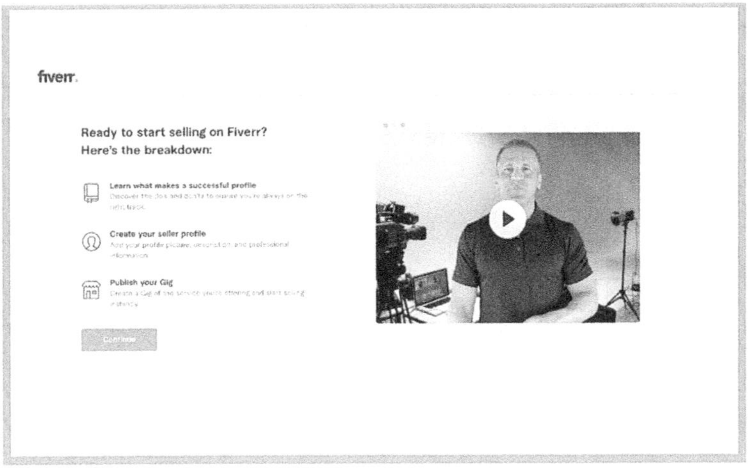

Source: Fiverr.com

It's now time to create your Seller Profile.

Your Fiverr Seller Profile is your personal branding page on the site.

It's where buyers go to learn more about you and your services, and it's also one of the first things buyers see when they search for someone to provide a service.

Because of this, it's important that you take the time to set up your profile and make sure it accurately represents who you are and what you do.

There are four sections to a Fiverr profile:

1. Personal Info
2. Professional Info
3. Linked Accounts
4. Account Security

Personal Info

Enter your full name below to get started selling services on Fiverr. Your original name will be kept private on your profile.

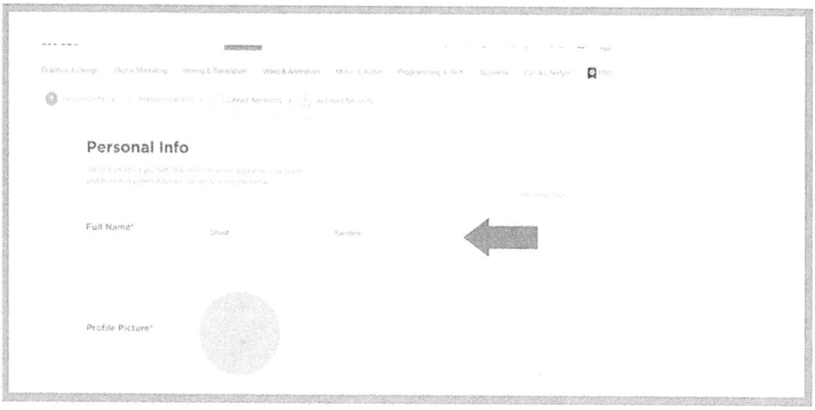

Source: Fiverr.com

Add A Profile Picture

Source: Fiverr.com

To add your profile picture, select the one you want to use from your computer. Keep in mind that everyone on Fiverr will be able to see it, so make sure it's an original photo that you have copyrights for. Buyers are more likely to engage with profiles that have friendly, recognizable photos. Do not use someone else's image, a celebrity's image, or an inaccurate photo of your service as your profile picture. GIFs will also not be accepted as profile pictures.

Describe yourself and your services

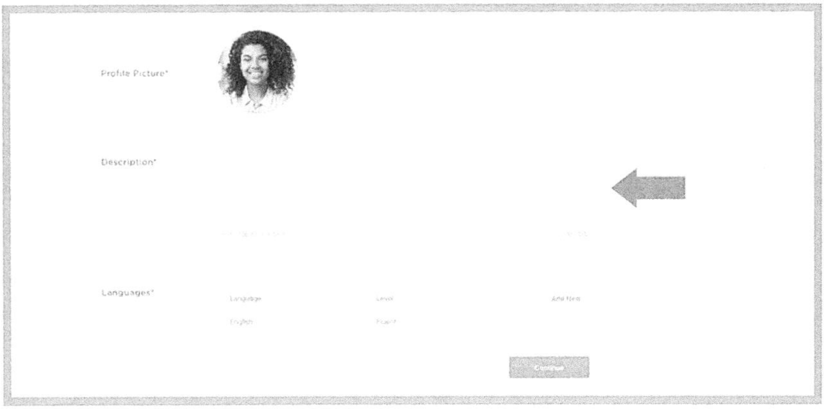

Source: Fiverr.com

This is your chance to introduce yourself to buyers and give them an idea of your services within 600 words. Be creative, but include relevant keywords so buyers can easily find you when they search for someone to provide a service. For example, if you're a web designer, you might want to include keywords like "web design," "graphic design," or "logo design."

Here are some tips for writing an irresistible profile description:

1. ***Keep it short and sweet***. Your profile bio should be concise and to the point - Buyers don't want to read a novel. They just want to know what you can do for them.

2. ***Use keywords.*** Include relevant keywords in your profile bio to help Buyers find you easily.

3. ***Highlight your unique selling points.*** What makes you different from all the other sellers out there? Tell Buyers what sets you apart and why they should choose you over anyone else.

4. ***Use persuasive language.*** Use persuasive language in your profile bio to convince Buyers that you're the best person for the job.

5. ***Be friendly and approachable.*** Let your personality shine through in your profile bio so Buyers can understand who you are.

6. ***End with a call to action*** in your biography, such as "Message me now to get started!"

Here's an example of a well-written Profile Description:

Hi, I'm Karen - a highly skilled and experienced SEO expert with over five years of experience in the industry.

I have helped several businesses increase their organic traffic and sales through effective SEO strategies, website optimization, blog content marketing, and more.

I am passionate about helping businesses grow and succeed online and would love to help you achieve your goals. If you're looking for someone who can help you rank higher in search engines and drive more traffic to your website, then I'm the freelancer for you. Contact me today so we can get started on your project.

As you can see, this description is clear, concise, and to the point. It tells Buyers exactly what Karen does, why they should work with her, and how she can help them achieve their goals. It also includes relevant keywords, such as *"SEO,"* *"traffic,"* and *"website."*

Finally, it ends with a ***Call To Action***. You have to assume that not everyone who reads your Profile is experienced with the platform. Many of them will be new Buyers. Therefore, you must tell them what to do when they've finished reading your Profile. In this case, the CTA is to contact Karen to get started on their projects.

So, let's review.

A good Profile Description should include:

1. *A concise description of what you do and what you can offer Buyers.*

2. *Keywords that will help Buyers find you more easily.*

3. *A highlight of your unique selling points.*

4. *Persuasive language that will convince Buyers to choose you over other sellers.*

5. *A friendly and approachable tone.*

6. *A call to action at the end, such as "Message me now to get started!"*

Select the languages you speak

Source: Fiverr.com

Make sure to select all the languages you speak and level of fluency.

Click ***Continue.***

Professional Info

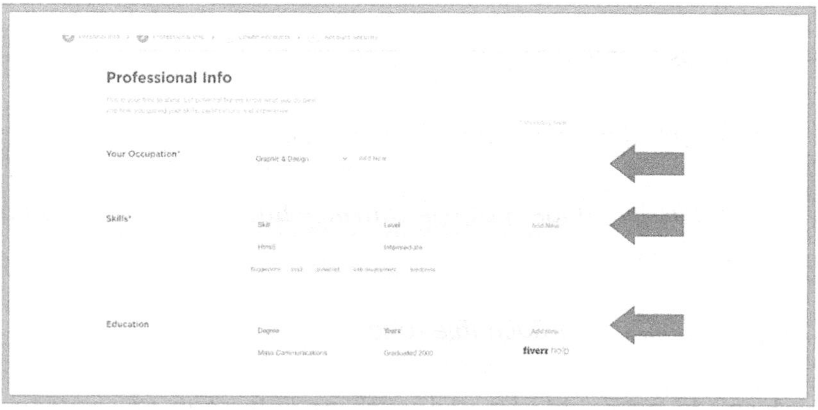

Source: Fiverr.com

Choose your occupation from the drop-down menu and choose how long you've been working in that occupation. Afterward, select which categories of services from Fiverr you wish to sell.

Next, add your skills and education to your profile. If you have a degree, add it, even if it's not related to the services you're offering on Fiverr. Buyers will be impressed, and it will show that you're a well-rounded individual.

If you have any relevant skills or experience, make sure to add them as well. These could include things like "Graphic Design," "Web Development," or " Copywriting." You can add up to 15 skills.

Source: Fiverr.com

If you have any certificates or a personal website, add them now. If not, don't worry about it. Click ***Continue.***

Link Your Accounts

Source: Fiverr.com

In order to link your Google, Facebook, and Twitter accounts, click the ***Connect*** button next to each social media account. This allows Fiverr to provide you with more business. Don't worry. This information will not be displayed publicly.

After you have connected all of the accounts, click ***Continue***.

Account Security

Source: Fiverr.com

You will need to verify your email and phone number so Fiverr can keep your account secure. Add your email address and phone number. Next, click Continue & Create Your First Gig.

Congratulations! You have now completed your Fiverr profile setup.

Now that you know how to set up your Fiverr profile, it's time to start landing some gigs! But first, let's talk a little about Fiverr Keyword research.

CHAPTER 6

Finding Keywords For Your Gigs

MOST NEW AND EXPERIENCED SELLERS DON'T REALIZE THAT Fiverr is a search engine that operates on rules similar to Google. This means that an AI (artificial intelligence) algorithm is used to determine which Gigs should be shown in search results.

To be successful on Fiverr, you want to ensure that your Gigs show on the first page of search results. You do this with Gig Search Engine Optimization (SEO) using the best keywords for your service.

What are keywords on Fiverr?

Keywords are words or phrases that a buyer might type into the search bar to find your service. You must use relevant keywords for your Gigs to show up in Fiverr's algorithm and attract buyers' attention.

Here's the number 1 way to find the best keywords for your Fiverr Gigs:

Use Fiverr's search bar!

Step 1: Switch your profile to Buying by clicking your Profile Picture and Selecting 'Switch To Buying.'

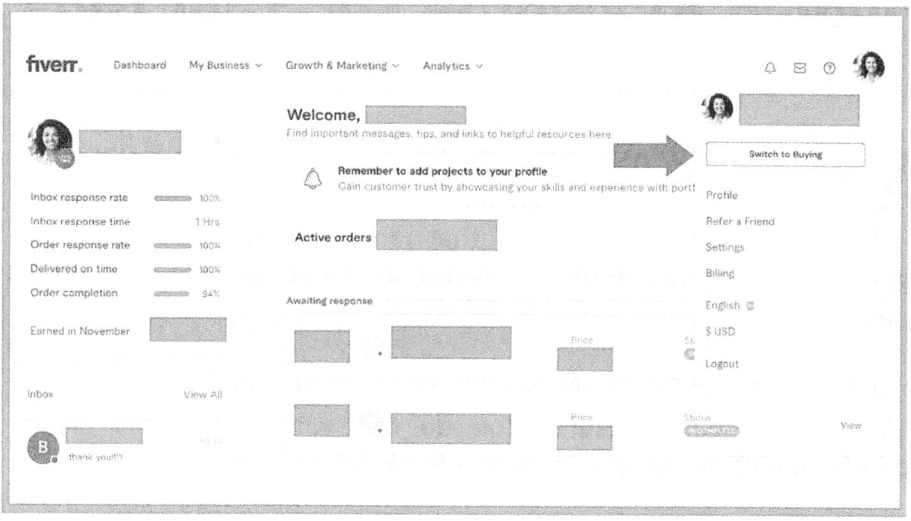

Source: Fiverr.com

Step 2: Switching will take you to Fiverr's Buyers' page. Type a generic service term in the search box and take notes of all the search terms that come up.

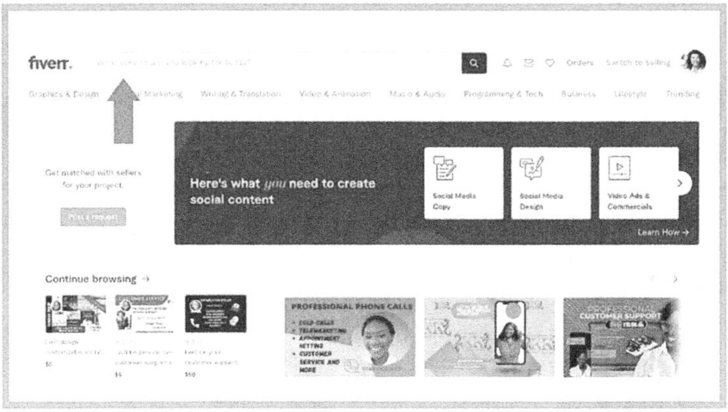

Source: Fiverr.com

For example, if I want to offer Virtual Assistant services, I would type 'virtual assistant' in the search box. Here's what comes up:

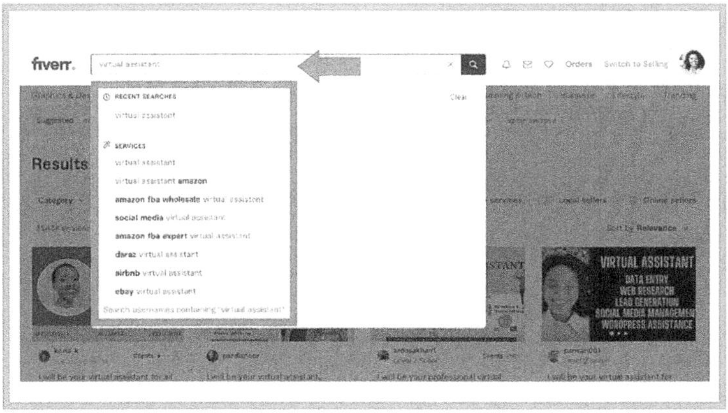

Source: Fiverr.com

Wait for Fiverr to show you all the related keywords below the search box and write them down.

Next, click on the one that's closest to the service you want to offer. I am going to click on the first term that comes up, virtual assistant.

This will take you to all the Gigs that have ranked on the first page for this search term. Change the default setting from Relevance to Best Selling.

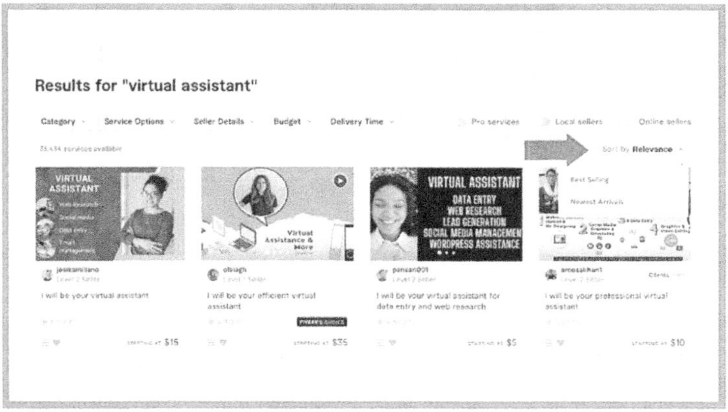

Source: Fiverr.com

Step 3: Click on any one of the Gigs on the first page and look through for the entire Gig, noting the keywords used throughout.

Source: Fiverr.com

Scroll to the bottom of the Seller's gig page and pay keen attention to the five tags used.

Write these down. You will be using these keywords when creating your gigs.

CHAPTER 7

Creating Fiverr Gigs (The Right Way!)

TO BE SUCCESSFUL ON FIVERR, OPTIMIZING YOUR GIGS IS ESSENTIAL.

Optimizing your Fiverr Gigs is important for several reasons.

1. It allows you to present yourself and your services in the best possible light.

2. It helps you stand out from the competition by highlighting your unique skills and talents.

3. Having a strong presence on Fiverr can help you attract more Buyers and close more sales.

Let's take it step-by-step and optimize each section of a Gig as we create it.

How To Create A Fiverr Gig

1. Go to your Fiverr dashboard and click on your Profile picture.
2. Select 'Create a new Gig.'
3. This page will pop up:

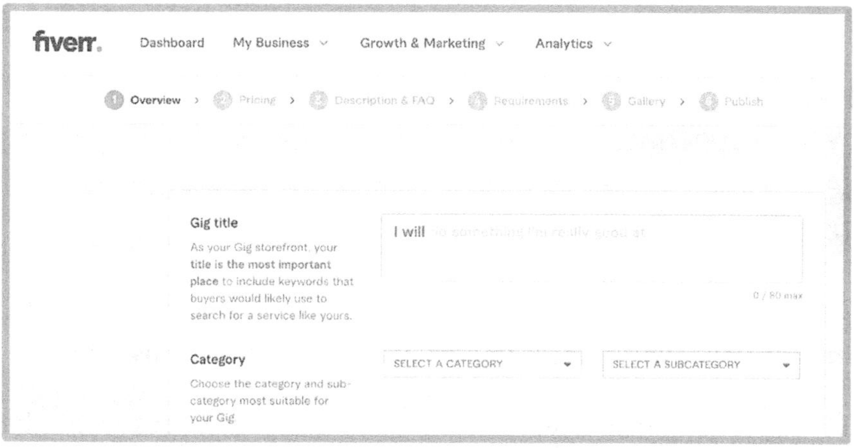

Source: Fiverr.com

You're now ready to create your first Gig.

Creating your Gig consists of 6 sections:

1. Overview
2. Pricing & Packages
3. Description & FAQ
4. Requirements
5. Gallery
6. Publish

Your Gig title, description, and tags appear on your Gig page and help convince Buyers to purchase your Gig. In other words, they're your sales pitch. And just like any sales pitch, they must be well-written and persuasive if you want to succeed.

Overview- Gig URL

Before we get into creating a fully optimized Gig Title, let's talk a little about the Gig URL.

Your Gig URL is the unique web address for your Gig page. Created from the Gig Title, it appears in your browser's address bar when someone is viewing your Gig. Many people don't know that this URL is also a searchable field on Fiverr and is unchangeable once you create a Gig. So, if you're not using keywords in your Gig URL, you're missing out on an opportunity to be found in search results.

To create an optimized Gig URL:

Using the keywords you found for the service you are creating the Gig for, write an SEO-optimized title without worrying about creativity or copywriting in the Gig Title section. It won't read well or make sense, but once the Gig is published, you will go back and change the title to a more suitable and grammatically correct one.

For example, I want to create a Gig for blog writing. The keywords I found included 'SEO blog writer' and 'SEO article writer.' I want to optimize my Gig URL for these two keywords. Therefore, I'll type 'SEO blog writer article writer' in the Gig Title section.

Source: Fiverr.com

I'll then continue creating the Gig and Publish. Once this Gig is published, the URL will be changed to "fiverr.com/username/seo-blog-writer-article-writer."

Source: Fiverr.com

Of course, the current title makes little or no sense to Buyers, so to fix that, I'll go back and edit the Gig Title to a grammatically correct, keyword-driven one.

Overview - Gig Title

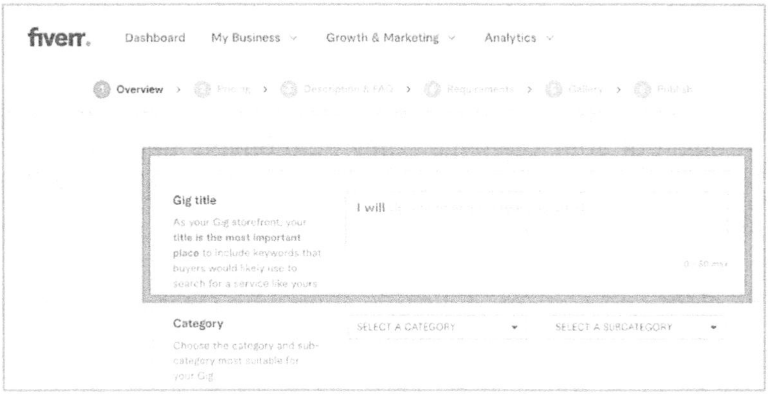

Source: Fiverr.com

Your Gig title is the most important part of your sales pitch. It's what appears in the search results, and it's the first thing Buyers see when considering purchasing your Gigs.

That means you need to make it count!

Fiverr starts each Gig title with *'I will'*. Sellers must complete this sentence in no more than 80 characters in order to create an effective title.

Here are some tips to help you write a compelling Gig title:

1. ***Keep it short and sweet:*** The shorter your Gig title, the easier it is for Buyers to digest. And the easier Buyers understand what you're offering, the more likely they are to purchase your Gig.

2. ***Use keywords:*** Keywords are essential in your Gig title and throughout your Gig page. They help Buyers find your Gig when searching for a specific service, and they also help you rank higher in the search results.

3. ***Be clear and concise:*** Your title should be clear and to the point. Buyers should be able to understand exactly what you're offering without having to read through a lot of fluff.

4. ***Use action words:*** Action words like 'create,' 'design,' 'write,' and 'optimize' are persuasive and help to engage Buyers.

5. ***Be unique:*** There are a lot of Gigs on Fiverr, which means you need to make yours stand out from the crowd. One way to do that is to be creative with your Gig title.

Here are a few examples:

- *I will design an amazing logo for your business.*
- *I will write an engaging and SEO-friendly blog post.*
- *I will create a stunning explainer video.*
- *I will optimize your website for better search engine ranking.*

As you can see, these titles are short, clear, and to the point. They use keywords and action words and are unique enough to stand out.

Overview- Fiverr Category and Sub-category

Source: Fiverr.com

Choosing the right category and sub-category for your Gigs is important because it helps Buyers find your Gigs more easily. It also helps improve your Gigs' ranking in search results.

When creating a new Gig, you'll be asked to select a Category and Sub-category. To ensure that your Gig is placed in the most relevant section, look at Fiverr's Categories before you create a Gig and choose the one that best describes your Gig.

There are currently 9 categories on Fiverr:

1. Graphics & Design
2. Digital Marketing
3. Writing & Translation
4. Video & Animation
5. Music & Audio
6. Programming & Tech
7. Data
8. Business
9. Lifestyle

Sub-categories:

Each category has its own set of sub-categories. For example, under the Graphics & Design category, you'll find sub-categories such as Logo Design, Photoshop Editing, and Illustration.

Having Gigs in several Sub-categories increases your chances of seeing more Buyer Requests and landing more sales (I'll discuss this later).

If you need help determining which category or sub-category to choose for your Gigs, you can always look at the Top Sellers with similar Gigs and see where they've placed them.

Overview- Gig Metadata

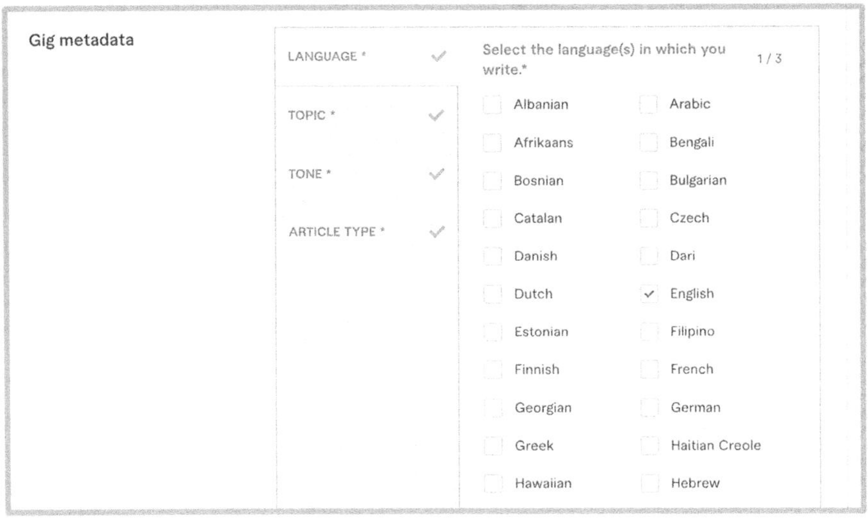

Source: Fiverr.com

Gig metadata are features that allow you to be more specific with the details of your Gig in the form of keywords.

Note: This is only available for specific categories.

Overview- Search Tags

Source: Fiverr.com

What are Fiverr Gig Search Tags?

Fiverr Gig Search Tags are the keywords you use to help Buyers find your Gigs. By using the correct tags, you can ensure that your Gigs show up in search results for the right keywords, making it more likely that Buyers will see and purchase your services. Fiverr allows up to five tags per Gig, so choose them wisely!

How can you find the perfect Search tags for your Gig?

1. The best way to find the perfect search tags for your Gig is to use Fiverr's Search bar. Type in some keywords related to your Gig, and see what comes up. You can also try different keyword combinations to see what works best.

2. Another method is to check out the competition. Look for Sellers within your Gig category, and see their tags. You can even use some of the same tags to help you rank higher in search results.

Make sure to keep your tags updated as your Gig evolves. If you add new services or features, update your tags accordingly. This will help ensure that Buyers always see the most relevant results when they search for Gigs like yours.

When you have selected your five tags, click ***'Save and Continue.'***

Now that you've completed all fields in the Overview section, it's time to move on to Pricing & Packages.

Gig Pricing & Packages

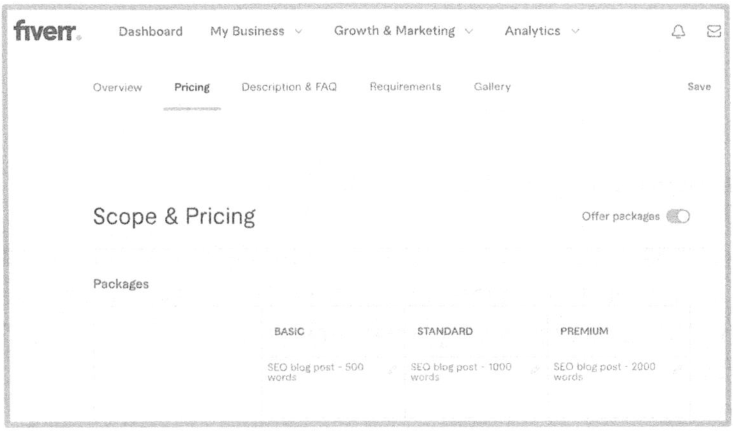

Source: Fiverr.com

One of the most important aspects of running a successful Fiverr Gig is setting your prices correctly. If you charge too little, you may not be able to make a profit. If you charge too much, you may not get any Buyers. So how do you set your prices?

Here are a few tips:

- ✓ ***Start with a low price:*** When you first start on Fiverr, it can be helpful to set your prices low to attract Buyers. You can increase your prices later once you have built up a good reputation.

- ✓ ***Be flexible with your pricing:*** Don't hesitate to offer discounts or special deals. This can help you to attract Buyers and get more sales.

- ✓ ***Consider offering extras:*** If you want to increase your prices, you can offer extras such as faster delivery or additional services.

Package those gigs!

What are Fiverr packages, and why use them?

On Fiverr, Packages are a pricing structure that allows you to bundle your core Gig with built-in revisions and Extras. This way, you can create an offer that gives Buyers precisely what they're looking for.

Packages enhance the Buying and Selling process on Fiverr in 3 ways:

- Packages make it easier for Buyers to find the perfect offer by giving them a variety of options to choose from.

- Packages give Buyers a sense of security, knowing they will get what they paid for.

- Packages allow sellers to increase their earnings by up to 20% by packaging their Gigs with Extras.

To activate triple Packages mode, go to the 'Create a Gig' page and click on the Pricing section. Then, toggle the button next to 3 Packages. From there, you can set how many upgrades and revisions you would like to include in that Package. Packages are automatically titled Basic, Standard, and Premium.

A savvy but lesser-known Fiverr SEO strategy is to have several packages available, with unique titles optimized for keyword rankings. According to Fiverr, its Premium package is the most popular option, so focus on making this particular offering as attractive as possible.

For example:

If you are offering Virtual Assistance and one of your keywords is 'virtual personal assistant,' your Gig titles could be:

- Virtual Personal Assistant 1 hr. (Basic Package)
- Virtual Personal Assistant 5 hrs. (Standard package)
- Virtual Personal Assistant 10 hrs. (Premium package)

This simple change in your Gig title could result in a higher ranking in search results and, consequently, more views and clicks.

When you're done, click ***Save and Continue.***

Description and FAQ

The Description section is where you tell Buyers what they'll get when they order your Gig. This is your chance to sell yourself and your services, so take some time to write a clear, concise, and compelling description. Use Bullets, highlights, or italics to draw attention to important information and address any common questions Buyers might have.

Make sure to include the following:

- A powerful hook
- A detailed explanation of what you'll do for the Buyer
- The benefits of buying your Gig
- Any relevant keywords or phrases
- A call-to-action

Here's my formula for writing a Fiverr Gig description that sells

Step 1: Write a powerful hook that grabs the Buyer's attention and makes them want to read more. This can be a statement or question that focuses on the problem your Gig solves.

Are you tired of struggling to get traffic to your website?

Step 2: Introduce yourself and state clearly what you do and how.

> *Hi. I'm Mike, a certified SEO professional with over four years of experience helping businesses increase their website traffic.*

Step 3: Get specific about your Gig's results and use social proof to back it up.

> *I've helped over 500 clients increase their website traffic by an average of 50% within 30 days. In some cases, I've gotten them to number one on Google for highly competitive keywords.*

Step 4: Explain exactly what the Buyer will get when they purchase your Gig.

When you order my Gig, I'll analyze your website in-depth and create an actionable plan to help you increase traffic. You'll also get a detailed report of my findings and recommendations.

> *I am:*
>
> *A Fiverr Level 2 Seller with over four years of experience*
>
> *An SEO expert with a proven track record*
>
> *Friendly and easy to work with*

Step 5: Add a call-to-action that tells the Buyer what to do next.

If you're ready to take your website to the next level, send me a message today and let me help you increase your website traffic and improve your Google ranking.

Including a call to action is important because it tells the Buyer what to do to purchase your Gig. Without a call to action, they may not know how to proceed.

Proofread your Gig description!

Make sure to proofread your Gig description for any errors or typos before you publish it. A well-written, error-free Gig description will help you appear more professional and increase your chances of making a sale.

You can use a free online proofreading tool like Grammarly to help spot any mistakes in your Gig description. Simply copy and paste your text into the tool, and it will highlight any errors for you. Then, you need to make the necessary corrections, and your Gig description will be ready to go!

It's also a good idea to ask a friend or family member to read over your Gig description before you publish it. Another set of eyes can help you spot any errors you may have missed.

And that's it! You now know how to write an excellent Gig description on Fiverr. Remember to keep your Gig description short, sweet, and to the point.

FAQs

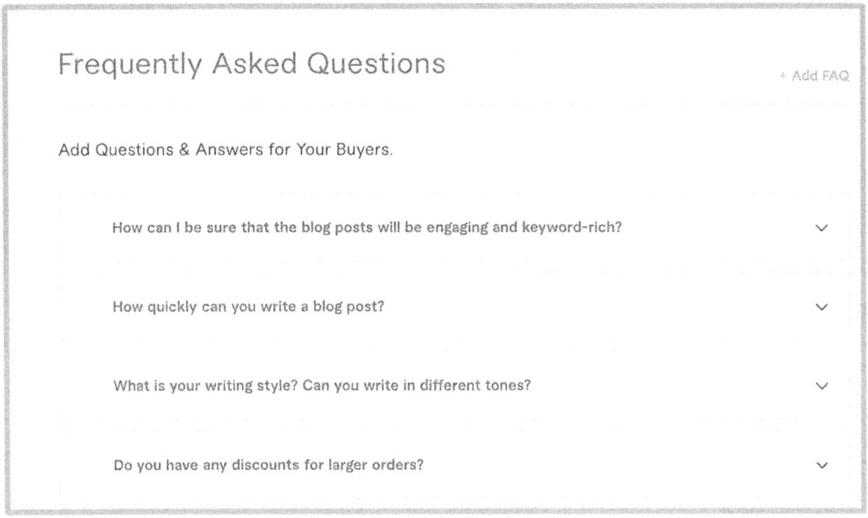

Source: Fiverr.com

The Frequently Asked Questions (FAQs) section is where you can address any common questions that Buyers might have about your Gig. This is also a great place to add relevant keywords or phrases.

To add a question, simply click the 'Add a Question' button and type in your question and answer.

Include your target keywords in the title of at least one FAQ question and its answer. By doing so, you will be optimizing your Gig to make it appear higher in search results.

Requirements

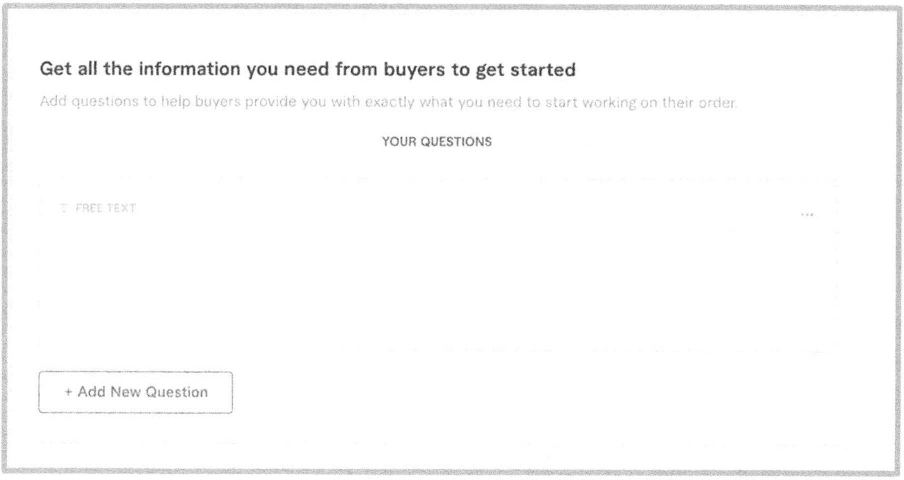

Source: Fiverr.com

The Requirements section is where you tell Buyers what you need from them to complete their order. This could be anything from a brand guideline to a storyboard.

If you have any requirements, be sure to add them here. You can also use this section to upsell your Gig by offering additional services that the Buyer might be interested in.

When you're done, click ***Save and Continue***.

Gallery

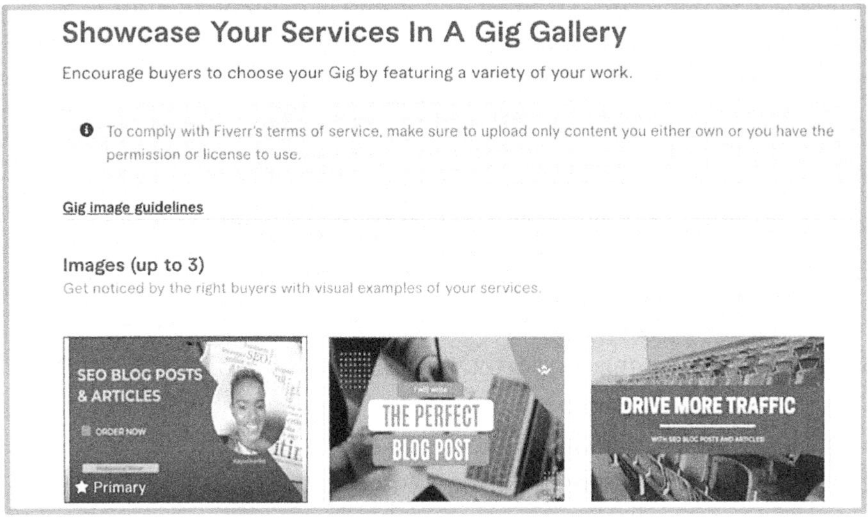

Source: Fiverr.com

For your Gig to be published, you must have at least one image uploaded to the Gallery. Fiverr allows Sellers to upload a maximum of 3 Gig images and 1 video (which we'll talk about later).

Your images should:

- Be high quality and clear
- Represent your Gig accurately
- Show off your work in the best light possible

Note: Fiverr does not allow pornographic, violent, or racist imagery. Your images must also adhere to Fiverr's Terms of Service.

How To Create Gig Images Buyers Can't Resist

Your Gig images are important because they're one of the first things Buyers will see when they come across your Gig. You want your images to be high quality and represent your Gig accurately so that Buyers will be intrigued and want to learn more.

Here are some tips for creating scroll-stopping Gig images:

1. **Use attractive visuals**

In business, your image is important because it will either make potential customers want to know more about your service or turn them away. If you have an appealing Gig, Buyers are more likely to click on it and actually read what you're offering. Your online presence should get people excited about what you have to offer so that you can generate revenue. Using attractive Gig images will reel Buyers in and lead to more sales and revenue.

For some, creating attractive Gig images may be a breeze. For the rest of us, we can use free online tools like Canva to create stunning visuals with no design experience or skills!

a) ***Sign up for a free Canva account*** *to start creating. Canva has ready-made templates for any design you can think of and boasts an easy drag-and-drop feature that makes designing a breeze.*

b) *Once logged in, click the 'Create a design' button and select 'Custom Size.' Enter 1280 x 769 px, then click 'Create new design.'*

You'll be able to choose from various images, so find one that fits your style and start customizing it. Canva has a library of built-in photos, illustrations, icons, and fonts that you can use in your design. Just click on the element you want to add and drag it into your design.

c) When you're happy with your design, save it using a keyword relevant to that Gig, for example, 'Travel blog writer.'

d) Then click on the 'Share' button in the top right-hand corner and select 'Download.' Then select the 'JPG' and 'Download' again. If you have multiple pages in the document, select the one you want to download. If you don't, all pages will be downloaded as a Zip file and will not contain the keyword you used to Save the file.

Pro Tip: Choose a different picture for each Gig image. This helps Buyers find what they need.

2. Keep it simple

Don't overcrowd your images with too much text or information. Stick to one main message you want to convey and make sure it's clear. You want Buyers to be able to understand what your Gig is about at a glance.

For example, if you're selling a writing Gig, your image might just feature some text that says, 'I write travel blogs!' with a photo of you in the background.

3. Include your keywords on Gig images

Your Gig images can make or break a sale. When Buyers search for services, they'll scroll through many images before deciding which service to purchase. Make sure your Gig images are clear, and relevant, and include your keywords so that Buyers can easily find what they're looking for.

4. Use people in your images

People are naturally drawn to images that feature others, so try to include a person or two in your Gig images. This could be a photo of you or someone else relevant to your Gig. You can find license-free images on pixabay.com, unsplash.com, and pexels.com

5. Don't use Fiverr logos or badges

Fiverr automatically includes badges with every Gig, so you don't need to worry about adding extra Fiverr logos, seller levels, or ratings. Any additional badges will be removed and could harm your chances of selling on Fiverr.

6. Don't share contact information

Do not put personal information on your Gig images—including contact information. This applies to both individual and business data of you or the customer, and all discussion should take place within Fiverr.

7. Use a call-to-action

Your Gig image is an excellent opportunity to include a call-to-action (CTA). A CTA is a statement or question that urges the reader to take action, such as 'Order Now.'

Your CTA should be short, sweet, and to the point. It should also be relevant to your Gig so that Buyers know what they need to do next. For example, if you're selling a social media marketing Gig, your CTA could be 'Get More Followers Today!'

8. Make sure your images are the right size

The images you upload to your Gig gallery should be 1280 x 769 px to look great on all devices. If your images are too small, they might appear blurry or pixelated when Buyers view them on a larger screen.

How to Supercharge Your Gig Gallery

Now that you know how to create awesome Gig images, let's talk about how to supercharge your Gallery section for greater visibility.

- **Include a Video In Your Gallery**

Did you know that Gigs with videos convert 200% more than Gigs without? So why doesn't EVERYONE have a video in their Gallery? Beats me! I know, however, that ALL the top Sellers have a video in their Gallery.

If you need help with making a video or what to say in it, don't worry! I've got you covered with a step-by-step guide on how to make an amazing video for your Gigs right here.

How To Make An Amazing Video For Your Gig

Firstly, you don't need expensive equipment, but you must ensure good lighting. Natural light is always the best but if you're not near a window, you can buy some inexpensive lights on Amazon.

Secondly, the audio is more important than the video, so ensure a good microphone.

Thirdly, you don't need to be on camera if you're uncomfortable with that. You can show your work or even do a screencast where you talk people through what you do as they watch your screen.

The maximum limit is 50MB and should be MP4 or AVI files. You're also able to set the desired frame for your video thumbnail.

Finally, just be yourself when it comes to what to say in your video.

Here's a breakdown of what to include:

- A very short greeting.
- Description of your Gig.
- Mention the details of the final output (if it's a logo, then talk about the resolution, size, and other necessary information)
- How much time you need to deliver
- Your packages and cost

- Make a note that your Gig is offered exclusively on Fiverr.
- Add music or voiceover to increase engagement.
- Don't use a computer to narrate your Gig—use your voice.
- End it with a call to action (CTA)

Pro Tip: Never include contact details in your videos. Fiverr will reject it and possibly ban you from the platform.

Here's what a script for a video like this might look like:

"Hi, I'm _______ and I offer ___________ services on Fiverr.com. When you order my Gig, you'll get ______ in return. And if you have any questions or need anything changed, just let me know, I'm happy to help.

I deliver all orders within _____ days and always aim to deliver early. My basic Gig starts at just $5, but if you need something more custom, I have some great extras that you can add on.

And remember, this Gig is exclusively offered on Fiverr.com so if you're looking for high-quality ________ services, look no further.

Go ahead and click that 'Order Now' button, and let's get started!"

As you can see, there's nothing too complicated about making a video for your Gig. Just be yourself, talk about what you do and what people will get when they order from you, and end with a CTA.

Helpful tips (by category)

Graphic & Design

- Upload images in all 3 image slots
- Use the 2 PDF slots to display more work (3 pages per PDF)

Digital Marketing

- Illustrations for Gig images should be iconic and elemental rather than detailed or "cartoony."
- Use a professional photo of the writer as an element of the main Gig image
- Make sure to set the delivery time to give yourself enough time to complete it
- Use a video of yourself explaining the service to instill more Buyer confidence
- Only show 1 certification badge in your main image
- Use the PDF section of the Gig gallery to build brochures about your service

Writing & Translation

- Use PDFs in the Gig gallery to display work samples
- Provide URLs to published online works
- Use a professional photo of yourself as an element of the main Gig image

Video & Animation

- Upload a video with sound for each Gig
- Use the Set Thumbnail option on the video to choose a still image for your Gig (from the video)
- Only use vertical videos for the Short Video Ads category.

Programming & Tech

- Illustrations for your Gig image should be iconic and elemental rather than detailed or "cartoony"
- Avoid using a screenshot of a website as the main Gig image as the detail is lost on the Gig card
- Only show 1 certification badge in your main image
- To list client websites, create a section in the description titled Client Work Examples, and do not use "www"
- Use the PDF section of the Gig gallery to build brochures about your service or display websites

Source: Fiverr.com

CHAPTER 8

3 Ways To Get Your First Client On Fiverr

- Buyer Requests
- Use the app to always be online
- Promote your Gigs

1. Buyer Requests:

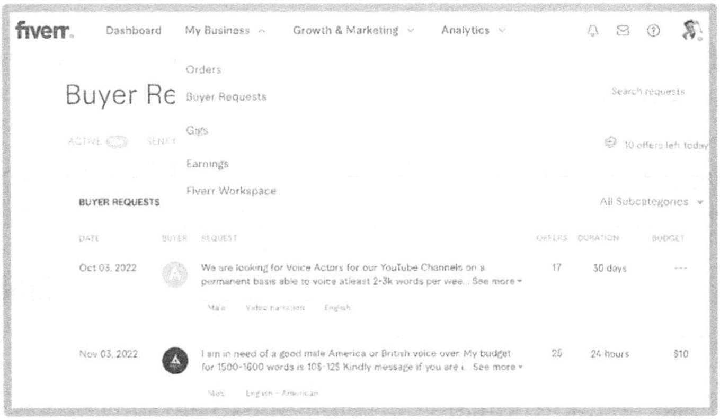

Source: Fiverr.com

One of the best ways to get your first client on Fiverr is by responding to buyer requests. These are open job postings that anyone can apply for, so it's important to make sure you stand out from other sellers. Make sure you read the requirements carefully and customize your proposal if needed. Make sure the buyer knows why you would be the best fit for their job and how you can help them.

To see Buyer Requests, ensure your profile is fully optimized and that you have gigs in as many sub-categories as possible. The more sub-categories you have, the more Buyer requests you'll see.

How to Use the Buyer Requests Feature

The Buyer Requests feature is available to all sellers on Fiverr. However, not all requests will be visible to all sellers. This is because requests are only shown to sellers who offer services that match the Buyer's needs.

For example, if a buyer posts a request for a logo design, only sellers who offer logo design services can see the request. This ensures that buyers only receive proposals from sellers who can actually complete the project.

To access the Buyer Requests page, simply go to the 'My Business' tab and select *'Buyer Requests'*.

On the Buyer Requests page, you'll see a list of buyer requests that match your gig sub-categories.

To submit a proposal, click on the 'Send Offer' button next to the request that interests you.

In the proposal box, introduce yourself and explain why you're the best person for the job. Be sure to include a personal message, as this is your opportunity to make a good first impression.

Once you've submitted your proposal, the Buyer will be notified and can accept or decline it. If your proposal is accepted, congrats! You've just won a new project.

Sellers can send up to ten offers each day. Use all ten, as this increases your chances of being hired.

And that's it! You now know how to use the Buyer Requests feature to win new projects on Fiverr.

2. **Use the app to always be online:**

You also should make sure that your profile is active on Fiverr's app. This will ensure that potential buyers see your Gigs when they search, even if you're not actively logged in. Make sure that you respond quickly to inquiries, as this will show buyers that you take your job seriously and value their time.

3. **Promote your Gigs:**

Lastly, be proactive when it comes to marketing yourself on Fiverr. Take the time to post regularly across social media platforms such as *Twitter, Instagram*, and *Facebook*. You can also reach out to other Fiverr users who have complementary services or similar gigs to yours, as they may be willing to help promote your gigs in return.

CHAPTER 9

Fiverr Seller Optimization Checklist

THE KEY TO SUCCESS ON FIVERR IS OPTIMIZING YOUR PROFILE, services, and strategies. To get the most out of the platform, you should use this optimization checklist as a guide:

1. **Profile Optimization:**

Make sure all information in your profile is up-to-date and accurate. Include keywords that buyers are likely to search for, such as your services and skills.

2. **Service Optimization:**

Have at least 7 gigs. Describe your gigs in detail, including what you offer, any specialties or unique features, estimated delivery time, and any questions buyers may have. Make sure to include:

- SEO Gig URL
- 5 relevant search tags per gig
- Relevant keywords in Gig title, description, pricing & FAQs
- 3 Packages per gig
- 3 High-quality Gig images in Gallery
- A video to introduce your services

3. Communication Strategies:

Respond quickly to buyer inquiries, be professional and friendly, and go the extra mile. Always follow through with orders on time, even if it's something outside of your services.

4. Marketing Strategies:

Stay active on social media platforms like Twitter and LinkedIn to reach more buyers. Utilize guest blog posts and forums to reach a wider audience.

CHAPTER 10

Your Fiverr Dashboard

THE FIVERR DASHBOARD IS THE FIRST PAGE YOU SEE when you log into your account. It's designed to give you an overview of your recent activity, earnings, and messages. It's important that you understand how to use the Dashboard so that you can make the most of your time on Fiverr.

This is what the Dashboard looks like to a Seller:

Source: Fiverr.com

On the left of the page:

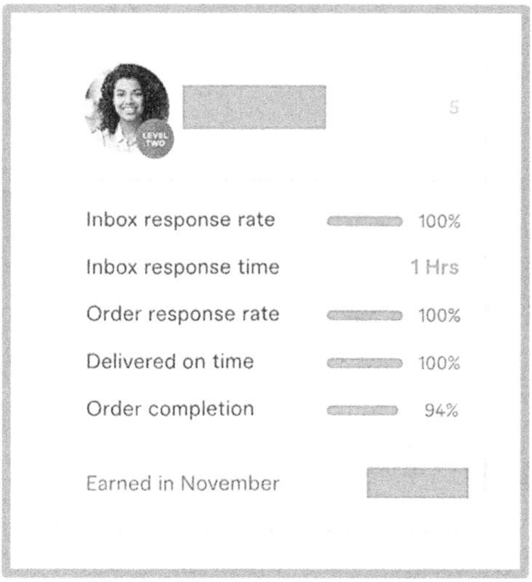

Source: Fiverr.com

- Your profile photo and Seller Level
- Earnings for the month
- Metrics

Metrics You Should Know:

- **Inbox response rate:** Answer at least 90% of your inbox messages over 60 days to maintain your level or qualify for the next one.
- **Inbox response time:** This is your average response time to inbox messages from new people in the last 60 days. The lower your response time is, the better.
- **Order response rate:** This is how often you answered order messages and revision requests within 24h in the last 60 days.

- **Delivered on time:** Deliver at least 90% of your orders on time for 60 days to maintain your level or qualify for the next one.

- **Order completion:** Complete at least 90% of your orders for 60 days to maintain your level or qualify for the next one.

- **Inbox:** Below your metrics, is your Inbox. Here, you can check all of your messages from buyers. This is also where you'll be able to send messages to buyers.

On the right of the page

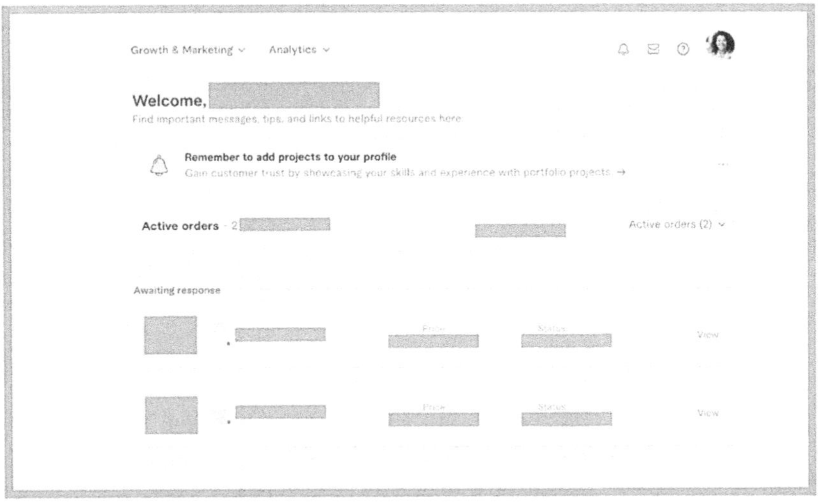

Source: Fiverr.com

To the right of your Inbox, you'll see a list of your ***Active Orders***. If you have any new orders, they will appear at the top of the list.

You can click on any order to view the details, including the buyer's requirements, the price, and when it is due.

Above your Dashboard, you'll see the ***Main Fiverr Menu***. This menu includes links to all the different areas of Fiverr.

Source: Fiverr.com

The first area on the dashboard is ***My Business***. If you click the drop down menu, you'll see:

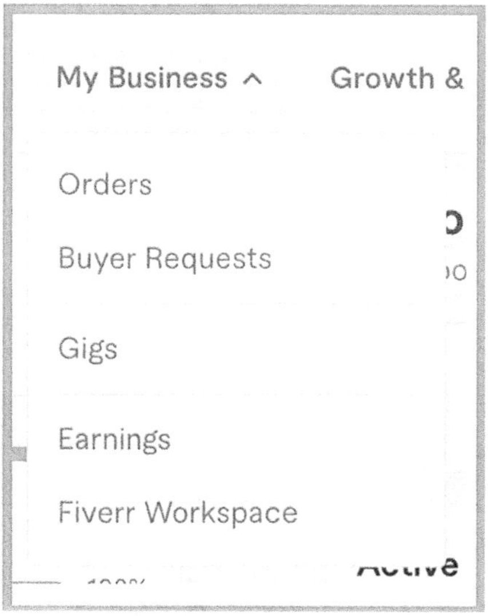

Source: Fiverr.com

- Orders
- Buyer Requests
- Gigs
- Earnings
- Fiverr Workspace

If you click on Orders, you'll see this:

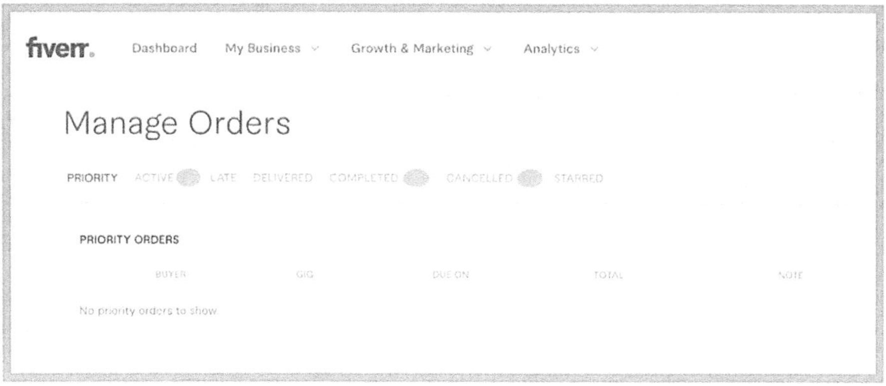

Source: Fiverr.com

Manage Orders

This is where you can view all your current and past orders, including canceled and late orders. You can also access your order page from the main Fiverr menu.

Buyer Requests

These are requests from buyers that match your skills and categories. You can browse through them and send proposals to the buyers. Fiverr recently changed Buyer Requests for some top Sellers to Matched! This means that rather than the Seller looking for Buyers, Fiverr sends tailored Requests to individual Sellers. The Sellers can choose to accept the tasks or not.

Gigs

This is where you manage your gigs. You can edit them, delete them, or create new ones.

Source: Fiverr.com

You'll see all gigs that are:

- Active (available to buyers)
- Pending Approval (needs approval from Fiverr)
- Requires Modification (need some changes before going live)
- Draft (not published yet)
- Denied (rejected by Fiverr)
- Paused (not available to buyers)

On this page, you can also view metrics for each Gig.

- **Impressions:** The number of times your Gig appears in a search result.
- **Clicks:** The number of times buyers clicked on your Gig.
- **Orders:** The number of orders you've received for that Gig.

- **Cancellations:** The number of all the canceled orders divided by the total number of orders on the gig.

Earnings

Source: Fiverr.com

On the Earnings tab, Sellers can view:

- **Net Income:** Your total earnings minus Fiverr's fees.
- **Withdrawn:** The amount of money you've withdrawn from your account.
- **Used For Purchases:** The amount of money you've spent buying other Sellers' services on Fiverr (we'll discuss this later)
- **Pending Clearance:** The amount of money you've earned that has not yet been cleared by Fiverr.
- **Available for Withdrawal:** The amount of money you have available to withdraw from your account.

Below this, you'll find Fiverr's payment methods:

- **PayPal:** You can connect your PayPal account to withdraw your earnings.
- **Fiverr Revenue Card:** This is a prepaid card that you can use to withdraw your earnings.
- **Bank Transfer:** You can withdraw your earnings to your bank account.

The Fiverr App

The Fiverr app is a mobile app that allows you to manage your account and gigs on the go. You can use the app to:

- Receive notifications when you get a new message or order,
- Respond to buyer requests.
- View your earnings and withdraw money,
- Share your gigs,
- Set availability (you can set yourself as unavailable if you need some time away from the platform)

Here is what Fiverr looks like on the App:

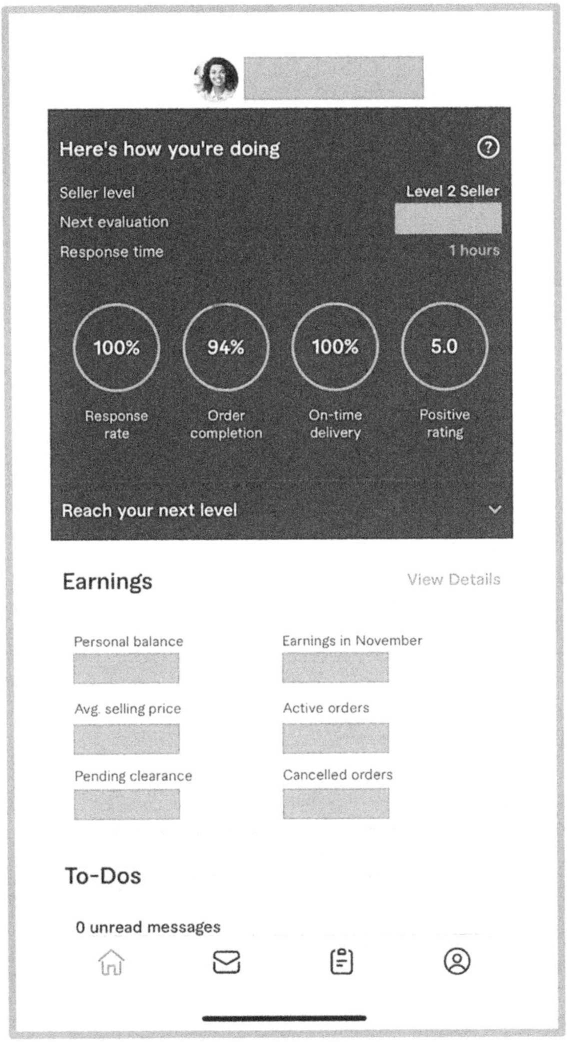

Source: Fiverr.com

CHAPTER 11

How To Upsell, Cross-Sell, and Make Bigger Sales From Your Fiverr Business

A**S A FIVERR SELLER,** one of the best ways to make more money is by upselling and cross-selling your services.

Upselling is when you offer a Buyer a more expensive version of the service they originally purchased from you. For example, if someone buys a basic logo design from you for $5, you could upsell them to a premium logo design for $50.

Cross-selling is when you offer a Buyer additional service that complement the service they originally purchased from you. For example, if someone buys a basic website design from you for $5, you could cross-sell them on an additional service like search engine optimization (SEO) or social media marketing.

You can make much more money from each Buyer by upselling and cross-selling your services. In this chapter, I'll show you how to do just that.

Upselling & Cross-Selling Your Fiverr Services

When upselling and cross-selling your Fiverr services, the key is to offer Buyers something truly valuable and worth the extra money.

Here are a few tips to help you do just that:

- ✓ Offer more than what they originally purchased. It's important to offer them more than what they originally purchased from you. If you're selling a basic logo design for $5, for example, your upsell should be for a premium logo design that is significantly better than the original.

- ✓ Make it an easy decision for the Buyer. It's important to make it easy for them to say yes. That means giving them a clear and compelling reason to purchase the upsell.

- ✓ Don't be pushy. You want to avoid coming across as a used car salesman trying to sell them something they don't need. Instead, you want to be helpful and offer them something that will truly improve their experience with your service.

- ✓ Use positive language. You want to sound excited about the upsell and make the Buyer feel good about saying yes to it.

- ✓ Offer a discount. If you're selling a premium logo design for $50, you could offer a 10% discount if they purchase it right then and there.

- ✓ Create custom orders. If you're having trouble coming up with an upsell or cross-sell that makes sense for your Gig, try creating a custom order. This allows you to work with the Buyer one-on-one to develop something truly valuable to them. Plus, you can set the price for that project however you'd like, allowing you to make some serious cash.

CHAPTER 12

How To Ensure Customer Satisfaction

ENSURING CUSTOMER SATISFACTION is essential to any successful business, especially when selling services on Fiverr. Here are 10 tips for keeping your customers happy:

1. Be professional in all communications – It's important to treat your customers with respect and communicate professionally at all times.

2. Respond quickly – Promptly responding to customer inquiries shows that you take their needs seriously and value their time.

3. Set expectations upfront – Make sure you clearly outline deadlines, delivery times, payment details, etc., so there are no surprises down the road.

4. Clarify instructions – Ask clarifying questions if instructions aren't clear to ensure that you deliver exactly what the customer wants.

5. Provide regular updates – Proactively keep your customer up-to-date on the progress of their project and let them know when any issues arise.

6. Respect deadlines – Meeting agreed-upon deadlines is critical for keeping customers satisfied, so make sure to plan accordingly and start work as soon as possible.

7. Offer excellent customer service – Always be friendly and courteous with customers, no matter how difficult the situation may seem.

8. Take feedback seriously – Listen to customer feedback, both positive and negative, and use it to improve your services in the future.

9. Be flexible when necessary – If customers need an extension or additional services, be willing to accommodate their needs whenever possible.

10. Follow up after delivery – Check in a few days after the project's delivery to ensure your customer is satisfied with the completed work.

11. Following these tips will go a long way toward ensuring successful collaborations and happy customers on Fiverr.

CHAPTER 13

How To Get More Positive Reviews, Fast!

AS A FIVERR SELLER, one of the best ways to get more Buyers and make more sales is by getting positive reviews. The trick is you can't simply ask for them. Fiverr prohibits Sellers from offering anything in exchange for a review, so you have to get creative.

Here are some methods that successful Fiverr sellers use to get more **positive reviews:**

1. Provide exceptional service - This one is pretty obvious but worth mentioning. If you want positive reviews, you need to give your Buyers a reason to leave them. Offer a quality service at a fair price and deliver it on time, every time.

2. Send a thank you note - After each transaction, take the time to send your Buyer a personal message thanking them for their business. This will help build rapport and show that you're grateful for their support.

3. Offer a bonus - If you want to go the extra mile, you can offer your Buyers a bonus for leaving a positive review. This could be something as simple as an exclusive discount on their next purchase or a freebie related to your Gig.

4. Follow up after delivery - Once you've delivered your Gig, don't just disappear. Send a follow-up message to ensure your Buyer is happy with the results. They'll be more likely to leave a positive review if they are.

5. Ask nicely - Sometimes, all you have to do is ask for a review. If you've done a good job and the Buyer is happy, they'll be more than happy to leave a positive review. However, since Fiverr frowns on requesting reviews from Buyers, you have to rephrase the ask.

Here's a script I use that gets me positive reviews every time:

Hi (client's name)

Thank you for the opportunity to provide (service) for you. Please see the attachments. I'd be happy to make changes if needed. If no changes are required, and you are pleased with the service, I would appreciate your positive feedback.

Thanks so much!

(Your name)

This simple message has a few key elements that make it effective:

1. **It's personalized** - I use the client's name to make it more personal and avoid sounding like a robot.
2. **It shows appreciation** - I'm thankful for the opportunity to work with the client and let them know it.
3. **It asks for what I want** - I'm very clear that I'm looking for a positive review.
4. **It's polite** - I say "please" and "thank you" to show good manners.
5. **It includes a call to action** - I tell the client exactly what I want them to do (leave a positive review).

By following these simple tips, you can start getting more positive reviews on Fiverr and improve your chances of making more sales.

CHAPTER 14

Promote Your Gigs To Get More Sales

MANY FIVERR SELLERS BELIEVE IN THE ADAGE 'BUILD IT, and they will come.' However, this couldn't be further from the truth regarding your Fiverr Gigs. If you want Buyers to take notice of your Gigs and make sales, you need to promote them actively.

There are several ways you can promote your Gigs on Fiverr, and in this chapter, we'll explore some of the most effective methods. By using a combination of these techniques, you'll be able to get your Gigs in front of more Buyers and start making the sales you deserve.

Let's get started!

1. Fiverr Gig SEO

The first method we will look at is Fiverr's Gig SEO feature. This powerful tool allows you to optimize your Gigs for the Fiverr search engine. Using the right keywords and phrases in your Gig titles, descriptions and tags makes it easier for Buyers to find your Gigs when they're searching for them.

2. Social Media Promotion

Another great way to promote your Fiverr Gigs is through social media. Having a strong social media presence can be a great way to drive traffic to your Gigs and make sales.

There are a few different ways to promote your Gigs on social media. One way is to simply share links to your Gigs on your various social media accounts. Another option is to create promotional images or videos for your Gigs and share them on social media. And finally, you can also run social media ads for your Gigs.

3. Blog Promotion

If you have a blog, this is another great place to promote your Fiverr Gigs. You can write blog posts that are specifically about your Gigs or simply mention your Gigs in your existing blog content. You can also include a link to your Gig in your blog's sidebar or in the author bio section at the end of each post.

4. Email Marketing

Email marketing can also be a great way to promote your Fiverr Gigs. If you have a mailing list, you can send regular emails letting your subscribers know about your latest Gigs. You can also include links to your Gigs in your email signature.

5. YouTube Promotion

Did you know that YouTube is the second largest search engine after Google? This means that there are always people looking for solutions to their problems on YouTube. And this also means that there is always relevant traffic for any Gig category you choose.

You can talk about your chosen topic on YouTube from both a Buyer's and Seller's perspective.

For example, if you sell blog writing services, you could create videos on the topic – How to write an SEO blog on (any topic). You don't have to talk about your Gig exclusively. Drop the link in the video description or add it to video cards. The fact that you have a Gig related to the video's topic will encourage Buyers to check it out.

6. Paid Advertising

Finally, you can also promote your Fiverr Gigs through paid advertising. You can do this through Google AdWords, Facebook Ads, and other paid advertising platforms. Paid advertising can be a great way to get your Gigs in front of more Buyers, but it can also be a bit costly.

So there you have it!

These are just a few of the many ways you can promote your Fiverr Gigs. By using a combination of these methods, you'll be able to get your Gigs in front of more Buyers and start making sales.

CHAPTER 15

How To Turn Your Fiverr Business Into A Full-Time Income Stream

IF YOU'RE ONE OF THE MILLIONS WHO WORK ONLINE as a side hustle, you've considered turning it into a full-fledged business. After all, what could be better than getting paid to do something you love?

Making the jump from part-time to full-time freelancing can be daunting, but it's not impossible. With some planning and hard work, you can make your freelancing career into a sustainable, full-time business.

Here are a few tips to help you get started:

1. **Create an emergency fund**

Before quitting your day job, it's important to set aside some savings in case of lean times. This will help you cover expenses and keep your business afloat during slow periods.

2. Define your niche

Defining your niche is the first step to making your freelancing business sustainable. What are you good at? What do you enjoy doing? When you know your strengths, you can start to build a client base that appreciates your skills.

You don't have to be an expert in everything, but you should be able to offer a unique perspective or skill set that sets you apart from the competition.

3. Build a strong portfolio

Your portfolio is your calling card as a freelancer. It's how you'll convince potential clients that you're the right person for the job.

Make sure your portfolio showcases your best work, and don't be afraid to experiment with different formats (including video and audio) to really show off your skills.

4. Get organized

As a freelancer, you'll wear many hats - from project manager to salesperson to accountant. It's important to get (and stay) organized, or you'll quickly become overwhelmed.

Invest in a good project management system, and learn how to use it effectively. This will help you keep track of deadlines, budgets, and progress so you can deliver quality work on time and on budget.

5. **Set realistic rates**

One of the biggest mistakes new freelancers make is undercharging for their services. When you're just starting out, it's tempting to lowball your rates in order to get clients.

However, this is a dangerous cycle to get into. Once you start working for low rates, it's hard to raise them later on. Instead, set your rates based on your experience and the value you offer.

6. **Market yourself**

As a freelancer, you're in charge of marketing yourself and your business. This means actively promoting your services to potential clients.

There are a number of ways to do this, including social media, networking, and content marketing. Find out where your target clients hang out online, and ensure they see you.

7. **Invest in your business**

Running a sustainable freelancing business is not a passive endeavor. You need to actively invest time and money into your business in order to make it grow.

This includes things like continuing education, attending industry events, and investing in marketing and business development tools. The more you invest in your business, the more likely it is to succeed.

8. Start networking

Networking is one of the most important things you can do as a freelancer. It's how you'll meet potential clients, partners, and collaborators.

There are many ways to network, both online and offline. You can start by attending events, joining online communities, or connecting with other freelancers in your field.

9. Diversify your income streams

Don't put all your eggs in one basket. When you're starting, it's tempting to put all your focus into landing that one big client. But what happens if they suddenly disappear?

Instead, diversify your income streams by working with multiple clients. Think of yourself not just as a Fiverr Seller, but a professional freelancer. It means you find clients anywhere online or offline. This will help to stabilize your business and ensure that you always have money coming in.

10. Invest in yourself

The best way to grow your business is to invest in yourself. Use some of the money you make to improve your skills, learn new ones, and attend industry events. The more you know, the more valuable you'll be to your clients. A great platform to use for this is Skillshare. Skillshare offers a massive range of online courses covering everything from graphics and writing to email marketing and SEO. The courses are super affordable and easy to follow, so you can learn at your own pace.

11. Hire help when you need it

As your business grows, you'll eventually reach a point where you can't do everything yourself. When that time comes, don't be afraid to hire help. This could be an assistant, virtual assistant, or even just someone to help with the occasional project.

Outsourcing will free up your time so that you can focus on growing your business and landing new clients.

12. Plan for slow periods

No matter how well you plan, there will always be slow periods in your freelance business. These are inevitable and nothing to worry about. The important thing is to have a plan for when they happen.

Start by setting aside some money each month into a savings account. This way, you'll have a buffer of cash to fall back on when business is slow.

Next, look at your marketing strategy and see any areas you can improve. You may need to be more active on social media or start attending networking events.

Finally, use slow periods as an opportunity to work on your business rather than in it. This is the perfect time to work on your website, create new marketing materials, or even take a break.

13. Take care of yourself

When working freelance, it's easy to forget to take care of yourself. But to be successful, you must be healthy and happy. Make sure you get enough sleep, eat a balanced diet, and exercise regularly.

You should also make time for your friends and family. Having a support system is important when you're running your own business.

14. Celebrate your successes

Remember to celebrate your successes. Running a freelance business can be tough, so it's important to take a step back and appreciate your accomplishments. When you reach a milestone, treat yourself to something special. This could be new equipment, a day at the spa, or a night out with friends.

15. Be patient

Building a successful freelance business takes time, so don't expect overnight success. Be patient and focus on taking things one step at a time.

If you're diligent and stay focused on your goals, you'll eventually achieve the success you're looking for.

Conclusion

CONGRATULATIONS! If you've followed the advice in this book, you now have the tools and knowledge to launch a successful freelance career on Fiverr. All that's left is for you to get started and make your mark.

This journey isn't always easy, so don't be discouraged if things don't happen immediately. It takes time to build a successful business and develop your skills. Just remember to stay focused on the goal and have patience.

I wish you all the best with your new career, and thank you for using The ***Fiverr Seller's Handbook: Easy Steps To Make More Money Online.***

Here's to many happy clients and profitable projects!

Sincerely,

Your Fiverr Buddy,

Kay

P.S:

Let's keep in touch!
kaywillwrite@gmail.com | IG: kaywillwrite | Blog: www.kaywillwrite.com

Karen Blair

'KayWillWrite'

Writer | Entrepreneur | Author

*** CONTACT ME TODAY TO LEARN ***

How to Make Money As A Fiverr Freelancer

~ Connect ~

* Fiverr: *www.fiverr.com/kaywillwrite* *

* Website/Blog: *www.kaywillwrite.com* *

* Email: *kaywillwrite@gmail.com* *

* LinkedIn: *@kaywillwrite* *

* IG: *@kaywillwrite* *

BIG BONUS!

Fiverr Gig SEO Checklist:

16 Fool-proof Ways to Optimize Your Fiverr Gig Listing for Better Visibility

1. **Find the right keywords for your Gigs:** The first step to Gig SEO is finding the right keywords. You want to ensure that you target keywords that potential buyers are searching for.

2. **Create a stellar Fiverr profile:** Your profile is your shop window on Fiverr. It's where buyers go to learn more about you and what you can do for them, so it needs to be engaging, informative, and keyword-rich. Use a friendly but professional image of yourself as your profile picture, and make sure your username is easy to remember and pronounce.

3. **Write an Overview that sells:** Your Overview is your chance to really sell yourself and your services. Think about what makes you

unique and what benefits you can offer buyers. Use keyword-rich language, and be sure to include a call to action.

4. **Optimize your Gig URL:** Your Gig URL is one of the first things buyers see, so it's important to ensure it's optimized for both users and search engines.

5. **Create an attention-grabbing Gig title:** Your Gig title is one of the first things buyers will see, so it needs to be catchy and keyword-rich. Use action words, and make sure your title accurately reflects the services you're offering.

6. **Choose appropriate Categories and sub-categories for your Gigs:** Selecting the right Categories and sub-categories for your Gig will help buyers find your Gig more easily.

7. **Add Tags to your Gig:** Tags are another way of categorizing your Gig and making it easier for buyers to find. Fiverr allows up to five tags. Ensure they are keyword rich.

8. **Offer and optimize Fiverr packages:** Giving buyers the option to purchase additional services or extras can help increase your earnings. The most effective way to optimize your Gigs is by creating three packages- Basic, Standard, and Premium. This allows you to utilize target keywords in the package titles as well as keyword variations in the descriptions.

9. **Make your Gig description clear and concise:** Your description is where you tell buyers what you can do for them. Be clear, concise, and specific, and use keyword-rich language. Include a strong call-to-action in your gig description to encourage buyers to purchase your services.

10. **Use the FAQ section to highlight what's included in your Gig:** The FAQ section is a great place to further elaborate on what buyers can expect from your Gig. Be sure to use keyword-rich language, and include relevant information to help buyers make an informed decision.

11. **Ensure you state the Requirements for each Gig:** This lets buyers know what they need to provide for you to get started. Fiverr will only allow a client to start the clock on a service if Requirements have been met. This protects you from having to start work without all the necessary information.

12. **Add multimedia to your Gallery**: Create Gig images using your free Canva account. Recommended image size: 1280 x 769 px (at 72 DPI). Upload up to 3 images that represent your Gig. Images can be samples of your work.

13. **Optimize your image file names and alt text:** When uploading images to your Gig, use keywords in the file names and alt text. This will help your gig images show up in search results.

14. **Add video to your gallery:** Videos are a great way to showcase your skills and services. Include a video with every Gig you create. You can use Canva to create high-quality videos without any video editing experience.

15. **Promote your Gigs:** You can promote your Gigs in several ways, including social media, email marketing, and paid advertising.

Your Notes

Your Notes

Your Notes

Your Notes

Your Notes

Made in the USA
Monee, IL
10 June 2024

59713004R00069